"There is no limit to what we, as women, can accomplish."
- Michelle Obama

Preface

Hello beautiful soul,

If you're reading this, chances are you're experiencing the weight of crushing debt and seeking a way out. Maybe you're feeling overwhelmed, helpless, and wondering how you got here. Believe me, I've been there. But let me tell you, you don't have to stay there.

I used to be in the same situation, constantly overburdened with financial stress. It was a constant source of anxiety, and I felt like I was stuck in a never-ending cycle of debt. Through dedication, hard work, and the guidance of experts, I managed to dig myself out of that hole.

That's why I'm excited to introduce you to "Broke No More: A Woman's Guide to Crushing Debt and Living the Life You Want." This book is a comprehensive resource designed to help women like us break free from the cycle of debt and achieve financial freedom.

In "Broke No More," you'll learn practical strategies for managing your finances, creating a budget, and paying off debt. You'll also discover how build your income and manage your broke mindset.

If you're ready to take control of your finances and crush your debt for good, "Broke No More" is the perfect guide to help you get there. I hope you find it as helpful and empowering as I did to write it.

Best of luck on your journey to financial freedom,

Karen

Introduction

Introduction

Hey, gorgeous ladies out there! Are you sick of living from paycheck to paycheck and feeling as if you're drowning in debt? Are you ready to take control of your finances and live the life you truly deserve? Well then, you have come to the right place!

Welcome to "Broke No More: A Woman's Guide to Crushing Debt and Living the Life You Want." I'm your fun-loving and sassy author, and I am here to help you get out of the financial rut and build the life of your dreams.

Let's be real: being in debt can be a total buzzkill. It can make you feel hopeless, overwhelmed, and stuck. But guess what, my friend? You are not alone! In fact, according to recent statistics, women are more likely to carry higher levels of debt than men. But here's the thing: It's not about how much debt you have; it's about taking action and making positive changes to get yourself back on track.

In this book, we will dive deep into the world of personal finance and debt management. But don't worry, I'm not going to bore you with a bunch of complicated financial jargon. Nope, we're going to have fun and break down these concepts in a way that is easy to understand and implement.

Together, we will explore practical strategies for managing your money, creating a budget that actually works, and finding ways to increase your income. We'll also tackle the emotional side of debt and how to overcome the negative mindset that often accompanies financial struggles.

But wait, there's more! This book isn't just about crushing debt; it's about creating a life that you love. We'll talk about setting goals, creating a vision for your future, and finding ways to live your best life without breaking the bank. We will then go on to talk about some ways that you can increase your income and change your thinking to allow more income to come your way.

So, if you're ready to say goodbye to being broke and hello to financial freedom, then this book is for you.

Let's do this, ladies!

Chapter 1: Building Your Foundation

| Chapter 1 |
Building Your Foundation

Hey ladies, let's be real. Managing finances can be tough, and the struggle is real. It's okay to admit it, and I am right there with you. I know that feeling in your gut, that sickening sensation when you have an expense coming up, but you're not sure if you can make it work. It can be stressful and overwhelming, but let's not dwell on the negative.

The good news is that there are steps we can take to get back on track and start feeling like we have more control over our finances. It's time to start living the life we want without the burden of debt and financial worries weighing us down.

Let's get real here: in order to start crushing your debt and living your best life, you need to face your financial situation head-on. And that starts with understanding exactly where you stand financially, warts and all.

Now, I know what you're thinking—tracking your expenses sounds about as exciting as watching paint dry. But trust me, it's one of the most crucial steps you can take towards gaining control over your finances. By keeping a close eye on your bills and receipts over a three-month period, you'll start to see patterns in your spending habits and identify areas where you can cut back.

Think of it like being a financial detective: uncovering clues about your money habits and using that information to build a solid plan for the future. It's not about beating yourself up for past mistakes, but rather learning from them and making positive changes moving forwards.

And here's the best part: once you start tracking your expenses and gaining a clearer picture of your finances, you'll feel a sense of empowerment and control that you may have thought was impossible. You'll be able to make informed decisions about your spending, prioritise your financial goals, and work towards creating the life you want.

First things first, let's take a look at your monthly expenses. It's time to grab your favourite pen and notebook and get down to business! Don't worry, this doesn't have to be boring. Think of it as a fun opportunity to learn more about your spending habits and identify areas where you can save some cash.

By tracking your expenses for at least three months, you'll have a clear picture of where your money is going and where you can cut back. Plus, once you have this information, you'll feel more confident and in control of your finances.

Now that you know exactly where your money is going, it's time to create a budget that works for you. The key here is to strike a balance between your fixed commitments, periodic commitments, occasional treats, and other monthly expenses. Don't be too restrictive, but also don't overspend and end up in debt. Remember, a budget is a tool to help you achieve financial freedom and live the life you want.

Start by listing out all your expenses, from rent and utilities to groceries and entertainment. Be detailed and honest with yourself about your spending habits. Next, allocate your income accordingly. This might involve some tough choices and trade-offs, but it will be worth it in the end.

Finally, remember that your budget is not set in stone. As your income and expenses change, you may need to adjust your budget accordingly. And that's okay! The important thing is to stay committed to your financial goals and adjust as needed.

Now, let's talk about setting goals. This is a crucial element of personal budgeting that should not be overlooked. Setting goals is not only a form of incentive to help you stay motivated, but it's also a way to create discipline that will prepare you for bigger commitments in the future. Whether it's saving for a down payment on a house or planning a dream vacation, having something to work towards will give you the motivation you need to stay on track. Setting goals will also help you gain a better perspective on the future possibilities of investment opportunities.

When you develop good financial habits, you're also developing skills that can be applied to your work, family life, retirement plans, and more. It's like hitting two birds with one stone! You're not just creating a better financial future for yourself; you're also setting yourself up for success in all areas of your life.

But let's talk about one of the most significant advantages of having a budget: avoiding debt. Debt can be a major source of stress and anxiety, and it can take a significant toll on your mental and emotional well-being. That's why it's essential to have a clear understanding of your expenses and income, so you can make informed decisions about your spending habits.

By following the simple steps I've outlined, you'll be able to gain control of your finances and make wiser decisions about your money. You'll learn how to track your expenses, create a balanced budget, and set achievable goals that will keep you motivated and on track.

Imagine a life where you're not constantly worrying about bills and debt, where you can actually enjoy the fruits of your labour and make meaningful investments in your future. This is not just a dream; it can be your reality if you take the time and effort to get your finances in order.

So, let's take charge of our finances and start building a brighter financial future, one step at a time. Remember, it's not just about the money; it's about developing the discipline and focus that will help you succeed in all areas of your life. You got this, girl!

Chapter 2: Creating A Budget Plan

| Chapter 2 |
Creating A Budget Plan

In this chapter, we're going to dive deeper into the exciting world of budgeting and how you can use it to make the most out of your hard-earned cash. If you've been following along, you know that tracking your expenses is the first step towards achieving financial stability. But once you've done that, what's next? The answer is simple: budgeting.

Budgeting is an essential tool for anyone looking to take control of their finances. By creating a budget plan, you can ensure that your money is going where it needs to go and avoid overspending or falling into debt. The first step in the budgeting process is to record all your income and expenses for at least three consecutive months. This may seem tedious but trust me when I say it's worth it.

Once you have a detailed record of your income and expenses, you can start incorporating follow-up measures into your budget plan. This is where the fun begins! There are several tools available that can help you with this style of tracking, including budgeting apps, spreadsheets, or even just a simple pen and paper. The key is finding what works best for you.

The next step is to record only the income and necessary expenses, such as commitments towards loans, insurance, education payments, and any other necessary bills. Ideally, these should be calculated as a yearly expense and then divided to fit into the monthly expenditure plan. This approach will give you a complete overview of your yearly commitments, allowing you to make payments in a more disciplined and affordable way.

Income refers to the money that you earn, whether it's from your job, investments, or other sources. Necessary expenses are the essential bills that you must pay, such as rent or mortgage payments, utility bills, groceries, and transportation costs. These expenses must be prioritised and paid before any discretionary spending.

However, it's essential to differentiate between necessary and discretionary spending. Necessary spending is defined as those expenses that are required for survival, while discretionary spending is defined as non-essential expenses such as entertainment, dining out, or shopping. Once you have calculated your yearly commitments, it's recommended that you divide them to fit into a monthly expenditure plan. This approach will give you a complete overview of your yearly commitments, allowing you to make payments in a more disciplined and affordable way.

The ultimate goal of budgeting is to ensure that your income is greater than your committed expenses. If this is the case, you can enjoy the leeway of adding on other expenses that are not deemed necessary or vital to your financial position. These may include little indulgences such as an occasional expensive meal or personal treat.

Though it's crucial to avoid overspending and falling into debt, While it may be tempting to splurge on non-essential items, it's important to stay disciplined and stick to your budget plan. It's also essential to review your budget periodically to ensure that you're on track and make any necessary adjustments.

Budgeting is an essential part of managing your finances effectively. You can achieve financial stability and make the most of your money by recording your income and expenses, incorporating follow-up measures, and prioritising necessary expenses. So, start tracking your expenses today and take control of your financial future!

| Chapter 3 |

Money Management

Spreadsheets are a popular and effective tool for keeping track of personal finances. They allow you to categorise expenses, create a budget, and monitor your spending habits. With a little bit of knowledge about how to use spreadsheets, you can easily create a financial management tool that works for you.

When creating a budget using a spreadsheet, it's important to first identify all sources of income and all necessary expenses, such as rent or mortgage payments, utilities, groceries, and transportation costs. Once you have a clear understanding of your monthly income and expenses, you can create a budget that takes into account your financial goals, such as saving for a down payment on a house or paying off debt.

Another option is to use money management websites or apps that automatically track your expenses and provide you with an overview of your financial situation. These websites and apps allow you to connect your bank accounts, credit cards, and other financial accounts, making it easy to keep track of your finances in one place.

Regardless of the method you choose, it's important to make sure that you regularly update your financial records to ensure accuracy. This means recording all expenses and payments and keeping track of due dates for bills and other financial commitments. By doing so, you can stay on top of your finances, identify areas where you may be overspending, and make necessary adjustments to your budget.

One of the benefits of using a spreadsheet or money management website is that you can easily track your progress towards your financial goals. For example, if your goal is to save $5,000 for a down payment on a house, you can create a separate category in your budget spreadsheet for this goal and track your progress each month. This will help you stay motivated and focused on achieving your financial goals.

Keeping track of your spending and financial commitments is a crucial step in managing your personal finances. Whether you choose to use paper and pen, spreadsheets, or money management websites, make sure that you regularly update your financial records and stay on top of your budget to achieve your financial goals. With a little bit of effort and organisation, you can gain a clear understanding of your finances and take control of your financial future.

Chapter 4: Managing Household Expenses

| Chapter 4 |

Managing Household Expenses

Managing our finances can seem like a daunting task, especially when we have multiple responsibilities to juggle. However, by taking a comprehensive approach and addressing all aspects of our household budget, we can ensure financial stability and work towards our long-term financial goals.

The first step towards creating a complete household budget is to accurately record all sources of income. It is important to include all income sources, such as a side business or part-time job, in addition to regular salary income. By listing all our income sources, we can get a better idea of our total income and plan our expenses accordingly.

Next, we need to list all the mandatory payments that are part of our monthly commitments. These may include rent or mortgage payments, utility bills, insurance premiums, and any other fixed monthly expenses. It is also essential to note any irregular payments, such as quarterly or annual bills, and average them out to include in our monthly household commitment budget. This gives us a clear understanding of the expenses that we incur each month.

After listing mandatory payments, it is important to allocate a budget for discretionary spending. This includes expenses such as entertainment, dining out, travel, and shopping. It is crucial to set a comfortable amount for these expenses that does not lead to overindulgence while still allowing us to enjoy some level of control and discipline over our finances. It is also important to track our discretionary spending closely, as it can quickly add up and impact our overall financial stability.

Savings are another critical aspect of a complete household budget. This includes setting aside a portion of our income for retirement, emergency funds, education, and any other long-term commitments. It is important to allocate a specific amount towards savings and stick to it, as this can provide a safety nett during unexpected events such as job loss or medical emergencies. By making savings a priority, we can ensure that we are working towards our long-term financial goals.

Finally, if we have any debts to pay off, we need to include the payments towards them in our household budget records. It is crucial to note the duration it would take to pay off such debts and add these payments accordingly. This will give us a clear idea of the debts we need to pay off and the duration it would take to clear them.

Creating a complete household budget that covers all these aspects may seem overwhelming at first. However, by taking a systematic approach, we can ensure that our finances are on track and work towards our financial goals with more confidence and control. It is important to review and update our household budget periodically, as changes in income, expenses, or financial goals may require adjustments to our budget. By taking a proactive approach to financial management, we can secure our financial future and achieve long-term financial stability.

Chapter 5: Negotiating Bills

| Chapter 5 |

Negotiating Bills

Living with debt is a reality for many people, but it doesn't have to be a permanent state. One of the ways to manage your finances and reduce your debt is by negotiating your existing bills and repayments with your creditors and service providers. When done correctly, negotiating your bills and repayments can help you reduce your monthly payments, lower your interest rates, and even eliminate some of your debt.

Here are some tips to help you negotiate your existing bills and repayments:

1. Gather Information

Before you start negotiating, it is important to gather information about your bills and payments. Review your bills and statements, understand the terms and conditions of your contracts, and identify areas where you can potentially negotiate. For example, you may be able to negotiate your credit card interest rates, phone or cable bills, or student loan payments. Gathering information is key to understanding your financial situation, which will help you negotiate more effectively.

2. Be prepared to negotiate.

Negotiating requires preparation and planning. Before you approach your creditors or service providers, decide on your goals and what you're willing to compromise on. Be confident and assertive, but also be willing to listen to their proposals and suggestions. When you have a clear understanding of your goals and priorities, you'll be better equipped to negotiate effectively.

3. Reach Out to Your Creditors

If you're struggling to make payments, reach out to your creditors and explain your situation. Many creditors are willing to work with you to find a solution that works for both parties. You may be able to negotiate a lower interest rate, a reduced payment plan, or a settlement to eliminate some of your debt. Remember that creditors want to be paid, so they may be willing to negotiate with you to make that happen.

4. **Consider Consolidation**

If you have multiple debts, consolidating them into a single payment can help you simplify your finances and potentially reduce your overall interest rates and monthly payments. Consider options like balance transfer credit cards, personal loans, or debt management plans. Consolidation can be a great way to reduce your debt and simplify your payments.

5. **Look for discounts and promotions.**

Many service providers offer discounts and promotions to retain customers. Be proactive and reach out to your providers to enquire about any available discounts or promotions. You may be able to save money on your phone or internet bills, insurance premiums, or subscription services. Keep in mind that providers may not advertise these discounts, so it's important to ask.

6. **Seek professional help.**

If you're struggling to negotiate your bills and repayments or feel overwhelmed by your debt, consider seeking professional help. There are credit counselling agencies, financial coaches, and debt settlement companies that can help you navigate the negotiation process and find a solution that works for you. These professionals can help you understand your financial situation and guide you through the negotiation process.

Negotiating your existing bills and repayments may require some effort and persistence, but it can lead to significant savings and debt reduction over time. By being prepared, proactive, and open to compromise, you can take control of your finances and live the life you want. Remember that negotiating is a skill that can be learned, so don't be afraid to practise and refine your skills over time. With time and practise, you can become a skilled negotiator and achieve your financial goals.

| Chapter 6 |
Emergency Funds and Other Savings

As we move towards a debt-free life, it's important to set ourselves up for financial success. This means planning for the future and creating funds that will help us reach our goals. One of the most effective ways to do this is by setting up bank accounts for emergency funds, travel funds, and other savings. In this chapter, we'll explore the benefits of these accounts and how to build them over time by putting small amounts away from each paycheck.

Emergency Fund Account

Life is unpredictable, and emergencies can strike at any time. This is why having an emergency fund is crucial. An emergency fund is a separate bank account that is solely dedicated to covering unexpected expenses such as medical bills, car repairs, or home repairs. The recommended amount to save is three to six months of your expenses. This may seem daunting, but by starting with small contributions, we can gradually build up our emergency fund over time.

How to Build Your Emergency Fund

Start by deciding how much you want to contribute from each paycheck. It can be as little as $10 or $20 per pay period. The key is to be consistent and to make contributions regularly. Set up an automatic transfer from your checking account to your emergency fund account each payday. This way, the money will be deducted automatically, and you won't have to remember to do it yourself.

Travel Fund Account

We all need a break from our daily routines and responsibilities from time to time, and travelling is an excellent way to recharge and rejuvenate. However, it can be costly, which is why setting up a travel fund account is a smart financial move. By allocating funds specifically for travel, we can avoid using credit cards or dipping into our emergency fund to cover vacation expenses.

How to Build Your Travel Fund

Start by estimating how much you need to save for your desired travel destination. Divide the total cost by the number of months until your trip, and you'll get a monthly savings goal. Add this monthly goal to your budget and set up an automatic transfer from your checking account to your travel fund account each payday.

Investment Funds Account

Another important account to consider is an investment fund account. This is a separate account where you can invest money for the long term with the goal of growing your wealth over time. Investment funds can include stocks, bonds, mutual funds, and exchange-traded funds (ETFs), among others.

Before opening an investment fund account, it is important to do your research and understand the risks involved. You should consider your financial goals, investment timeframe, and risk tolerance before making any investments. It is also recommended that you seek advice from a financial advisor to help guide your investment decisions.

How to Build Your Investment Fund Account

Once you have opened an investment fund account, you can start contributing small amounts from each paycheck to it. As with the other accounts, consistency is key. Even if you can only afford to contribute a small amount each month, it can add up over time, especially with the power of compound interest.

Other Savings Accounts

Apart from emergency and travel funds, there are other savings accounts that can help us reach our financial goals. Some examples include retirement accounts, education funds, and home-buying funds.

How to Build Your Other Savings Accounts

Determine how much you need to save and divide it by the number of months you need to reach your goal. Add this monthly goal to your budget and set up an automatic transfer from your checking account to your savings account each payday.

Creating bank accounts for emergency funds, travel funds, and other savings is an essential step towards financial freedom. By contributing small amounts from each paycheck, we can gradually build up these funds and have a safety net for unexpected expenses and future goals. Remember to stay consistent and make contributions regularly to ensure the success of your savings plan.

Chapter 7: Creating Wealth Through Investments

| Chapter 7 |

Creating Wealth Through Investments

Personal finance is an essential aspect of our lives, and investing our money wisely is one of the best ways to secure our financial future. However, many people may find the idea of investing their money overwhelming or confusing. In this chapter, we will delve deeper into personal finance and discuss how to invest our money wisely to secure our financial future.

1. Personal Savings Plan

Personal savings plans can be an excellent source of income in the future. However, it's important to enforce a committed savings plan where access to the funds is limited or non-existent. This will ensure that you don't dip into your savings for unnecessary expenses or emergencies. One way to enforce this is by creating a separate savings account that is only for emergency funds or long-term savings. This account should not be used for day-to-day expenses, and you should only withdraw from it in the case of an emergency.

2. Diversify Your Portfolio

Having a diversified portfolio of financial investments is crucial to minimising risk and maximising future income. Look into investing in a variety of options, such as stocks, bonds, real estate, and mutual funds. This way, if one investment doesn't perform well, you have others to fall back on. Diversification can help you mitigate risks and provide a better return on investment. You should also ensure that you are investing in reputable companies or organisations to avoid scams or fraud.

3. Long-term Investments

While short-term investments may seem appealing, they often provide lower earning possibilities compared to long-term investments. Consider investing in government bonds, insurance policies, or bonds from reputable agencies and establishments to ensure a steady source of income in the long run. These types of investments can provide a stable income stream, and they also have lower risk levels compared to other investments.

4. Know Your Risk Tolerance

It's crucial to assess your primary risk tolerance before investing. Every individual has a different level of risk tolerance, and it's essential to understand what you are comfortable with. While high-risk investments can provide a higher return, they also come with a higher chance of loss. On the other hand, low-risk investments may not provide as high a return, but they are safer. Choose investments that align with your risk tolerance to avoid financial stress.

5. Consider The Tax Implications

Before investing, make sure to calculate the relevant tax incurring ratios to ensure the investment is worth venturing into. This will prevent any unexpected tax liabilities in the future. Tax implications can significantly impact your returns, and it's essential to consider them before investing. Consult with a tax professional to better understand the tax implications of your investments.

It's important to note that investing your money wisely takes time and effort, but it's worth it in the end. The key is to start small and gradually increase your investments as you become more comfortable with the process. Don't be discouraged if your investments don't yield returns immediately, as investments often take time to mature. It's essential to have patience and persistence when it comes to investing.

Investing your money wisely can be an excellent way to secure your financial future. Personal savings plans, diversification, long-term investments, knowing your risk tolerance, and considering tax implications are some of the essential factors to consider when investing your money. By following these tips and taking a long-term approach to your investments, you can build a portfolio that provides a stable income stream and secures your financial future.

| Chapter 8 |

Planning For Retirement

Retirement is a significant milestone in life that requires careful planning and preparation. It is a time when one stops working and their main source of income shifts from active employment to other sources like savings, investments, or pensions. As women, it's crucial to plan for our retirement to secure our financial future, maintain our standard of living, and achieve financial freedom.

Retirement planning involves taking a closer look at your current financial situation, evaluating your goals, and determining how much money you'll need to live comfortably during your golden years. Here are some key steps to consider when planning for retirement:

1. Start early: The earlier you start saving for retirement, the better off you will be. Starting early gives you more time to build your savings and investments, which can compound over time. If you're young, take advantage of your employer's retirement plan or open your own independent superannuation fund to start saving for your future.

2. Determine your retirement income needs: You'll need to estimate your retirement income needs based on your lifestyle, expected expenses, and inflation. Consider factors like housing, healthcare, travel, and leisure activities. Don't forget to factor in unexpected expenses like medical emergencies or major repairs.

3. Invest wisely: A well-diversified investment portfolio can help you grow your retirement savings over time. Consider investing in stocks, bonds, mutual funds, or exchange-traded funds (ETFs). Keep in mind that investment returns are not guaranteed, so it's essential to work with a financial advisor or do your research before investing.

4. Debt reduction can help you save more for retirement and improve your overall financial stability. Pay off high-interest debt like credit cards or loans as soon as possible to avoid accumulating unnecessary interest charges.

5. Consider international retirement options: While many countries offer retirement plans, there are also retirement-friendly countries that offer tax benefits and other incentives to foreign retirees. Consider researching and exploring options for international retirement if it aligns with your goals and aspirations.

6. Have a contingency plan: life is unpredictable, and it's important to have a plan B in case of emergencies. Consider having an emergency fund that can cover unexpected expenses or creating a plan that allows you to continue generating income even after you retire.

Retirement planning is a continuous process, and you should regularly review and adjust your plan based on changes in your life, financial situation, and economic conditions. By starting early, investing wisely, minimising debt, and having a contingency plan, you can enjoy a comfortable retirement and live the life you want.

Chapter 9: Building Your Income

| Chapter 9 |

Building Your Income

In addition to managing our expenses and budget, it's essential to focus on building our income to achieve long-term financial stability. In this chapter, we will explore some strategies to increase our income and reach our financial goals.

1. Negotiate Your Salary

Negotiating your salary is an important part of building your income, and it's a skill that can be learned and honed with practise. Many women feel hesitant to negotiate their salaries, often out of fear of appearing greedy or aggressive. However, it's important to remember that negotiating your salary is not about being greedy or aggressive but rather about securing fair compensation for your hard work and contributions.

One of the first steps to negotiating your salary is to do your research. Before entering into salary negotiations, take the time to research industry standards and the salary range for your position. This will give you a clear idea of what to expect and what you can reasonably ask for. Many online resources can help with this research, such as industry-specific websites, job boards, and salary surveys.

Once you have a clear understanding of the salary range for your position, it's important to assess your value to the company. Consider your skills, experience, and the unique contributions you bring to the company. Be prepared to articulate your value clearly and confidently during salary negotiations.

When it comes to negotiating your salary, preparation is key. Take the time to create a plan and practise your negotiation strategy. This can involve rehearsing your talking points with a trusted friend or mentor or role-playing negotiations with a colleague.

During the negotiation, remain confident and assertive, but also be willing to listen and respond to the employer's concerns. Remember to focus on the value you bring to the company and how a higher salary will benefit both you and the organisation.

Finally, be prepared to compromise if necessary. While it's important to aim for a higher salary, it's also important to be realistic and open to finding a mutually beneficial solution. Consider alternative forms of compensation, such as flexible work arrangements or additional benefits, that may be valuable to you.

Negotiating your salary can be a daunting task, but it's an essential part of building your income and securing fair compensation for your hard work. By researching industry standards, assessing your value to the company, and preparing a strong negotiation strategy, you can successfully negotiate a higher salary and take control of your financial future.

2. Pursue Additional Education and Training

Continued education and professional development are essential to thriving in today's job market. By investing in ourselves and expanding our skill set, we become more valuable to our employers and can increase our earning potential. Pursuing additional education and training can also open up new career opportunities and help us stay up-to-date with the latest trends and technologies in our field.

One way to pursue additional education is by taking online courses. Many universities and colleges offer online courses that can be taken at our own pace and fit into our busy schedules. These courses can range from short-term skill-building courses to full degree programmes. Online courses can be a cost-effective way to learn new skills or gain additional qualifications while continuing to work.

Attending workshops or conferences is another way to gain new knowledge and skills. These events provide opportunities to network with other professionals in our field and learn from experts in our industry. Workshops and conferences can also offer hands-on learning experiences that allow us to practise and apply new skills in a supportive environment.

Pursuing a degree or certification in our field can also lead to increased earning potential and career advancement. A degree or certification demonstrates our commitment to our profession and shows that we have the knowledge and skills to excel in our field. In some industries, certain certifications are required to advance to higher-level positions or work with specific clients or projects.

It's important to note that pursuing additional education and training can come at a financial cost. However, it's important to view it as an investment in ourselves and our future. We can research financial aid options or speak with our employer about tuition reimbursement programmes to help offset the cost. It's also important to weigh the potential return on investment and consider the long-term benefits of pursuing additional education.

Pursuing additional education and professional development can provide opportunities for career advancement and increased earning potential. Online courses, workshops, conferences, and pursuing a degree or certification are all viable options to consider. By investing in ourselves and expanding our skill set, we become more valuable to our employers and can achieve greater financial success in our careers.

3. Start a Side Business or Freelance Work

Starting a side business or doing freelance work can be a great way to supplement your income and take control of your financial situation. With the rise of the gig economy and the availability of online platforms, it's now easier than ever to turn your skills or interests into a profitable venture. Here are some tips for starting a successful side business or doing freelance work:

a) Identify your skills and interests: Before starting your side business or freelancing, it's important to identify your skills and interests. What are you good at? What do you enjoy doing? This will help you determine what type of business or service to offer and will make the work more enjoyable.

b) Research your market: Once you have identified your skills and interests, research the market to determine if there is a demand for your services or products. Look for gaps in the market that you can fill or ways to improve on existing offerings.

c) Develop a business plan: Develop a business plan that outlines your goals, target market, pricing strategy, marketing plan, and financial projections. This will help you stay focused and on track as you build your business.

d) Build your online presence: In today's digital age, having a strong online presence is crucial for any business or freelancer. Build a website, create social media profiles, and use online platforms to showcase your work and attract clients.

e) Set your rates: Determine your rates based on your skills and experience, the market demand, and the value you offer. Be mindful of pricing yourself too low or too high, as this can impact your perceived value and affect your earning potential.

f) Network and market yourself: As a freelancer or small business owner, it's important to network and market yourself to attract clients and grow your business. Attend industry events, join online communities, and use social media to build relationships and showcase your work.

Starting a side business or freelancing may require some initial investment and effort, but it can pay off in the long run. By leveraging your skills and interests, researching your market, developing a business plan, building your online presence, setting your rates, and networking and marketing yourself, you can build a successful and profitable side business or freelancing career.

4. Invest in Yourself

Investing in yourself is a crucial step in building your income and achieving your financial goals. When you invest in yourself, you prioritise personal and professional development, learn new skills, and create opportunities for career growth and increased earning potential. Here are some ways you can invest in yourself:

a) Personal Development: Personal development involves working on your mindset, mental health, and emotional intelligence. This could involve practising mindfulness, meditation, or therapy. When you invest in your personal development, you become more self-aware, which helps you identify and overcome limiting beliefs and self-doubt. You become more confident and resilient, which can help you navigate challenges and take risks in your career.

b) Learning New Skills: In today's fast-paced job market, staying up-to-date with the latest trends and technologies is crucial to remaining competitive. Pursuing additional education and training can provide opportunities for career advancement and increased earning potential. Consider taking online courses, attending workshops or conferences, or pursuing a degree or certification in your field. This can help you acquire new skills, enhance your expertise, and become more valuable to potential employers or clients.

c) Networking: Building relationships with others in your industry can provide opportunities for career growth and increased earning potential. Joining professional organisations, attending networking events, and connecting with others on social media platforms like LinkedIn can help you build your network. This can lead to new job opportunities, collaborations, and potential clients or customers for your side business.

d) Investing in Your Health: Taking care of your health can help you stay focused, energised, and productive, which can translate into increased income. This could involve eating healthy, exercising regularly, and getting enough sleep. When you invest in your health, you become more resilient and less likely to burn out, which can help you stay focused on your career goals.

Investing in yourself is a crucial step in building your income and achieving your financial goals. By prioritising personal and professional development, learning new skills, building your network, and taking care of your health, you can create opportunities for career growth and increased earning potential.

5. Explore Passive Income Streams

Passive income is a type of income that is earned without the need for constant or direct involvement. Unlike traditional income sources like salary or hourly wages, passive income is typically earned through investments or ongoing businesses that require minimal effort to maintain.

One way to build passive income streams is through rental income. Owning a rental property or properties can provide a steady stream of income each month. However, it requires an initial investment of money and time to find and purchase a property, as well as managing the property, finding tenants, and ensuring that the property is well-maintained. Despite the initial effort, rental income can provide a significant source of passive income for years to come.

Another way to build passive income streams is through investments. Investing in stocks, bonds, mutual funds, or other types of securities can provide a steady stream of income through dividends or interest payments. While investing requires some initial research and effort to identify the right investments, it can provide long-term financial stability and growth.

Investing in real estate through Real Estate Investment Trusts (REITs) is another option for building passive income. REITs allow investors to pool their money together to purchase and manage real estate properties. Investors receive dividends based on the profits earned by the properties owned by the REIT.

Creating and selling digital products or online courses can also be a way to generate passive income. Once the product or course is created, it can be sold multiple times without requiring additional effort. This type of passive income requires effort upfront to create the product, but it can provide long-term financial stability and freedom.

Building passive income streams requires some initial investment or effort, but it can provide long-term financial stability and freedom. Passive income can supplement your primary income source, providing financial security and allowing you to achieve your financial goals.

6. Explore Online Passive Income Streams

The internet has opened up numerous opportunities for the exploration of online digital passive income streams to earn extra income. The beauty of digital passive income is that it can be generated from anywhere, as long as you have an internet connection and a computer or smartphone.

One way to earn passive income online is through affiliate marketing. This involves promoting other people's products and services through a unique affiliate link. When someone clicks on your link and makes a purchase, you earn a commission. Affiliate marketing can be done through a blog, social media, or email marketing. It's important to choose products or services that align with your audience's interests and needs to increase the likelihood of making sales.

Another digital passive income stream is creating and selling digital products. This could involve creating an ebook, online course, or digital product such as a template or printable. Once you've created the product, it can be sold on platforms such as Etsy, Amazon, or your own website. Creating and selling digital products allows you to leverage your expertise and interests to generate income while also helping others.

Creating and monetising a blog or YouTube channel can also be a source of passive income. This could involve creating content on a topic you're passionate about, building an audience, and then monetising through advertising, sponsorships, or affiliate marketing. While building a following can take time and effort, it can provide long-term passive income.

Finally, online tutoring or coaching can also be a source of passive income. This could involve creating online courses or offering coaching services through platforms such as Zoom or Skype. By leveraging your expertise, you can create a source of passive income while also helping others achieve their goals.

The internet provides numerous opportunities for women to explore digital passive income streams to earn extra income. Whether it's through affiliate marketing, creating digital products, blogging, or coaching, there are options for every interest and skill set. While building passive income streams may require some initial effort, the long-term financial stability and freedom it provides can be worth the investment.

Building your income takes time and effort, but it's worth it in the long run. By focusing on negotiating your salary, pursuing additional education and training, starting a side business, investing in yourself, and exploring passive income streams, you can increase your income and achieve your financial goals. Remember to be patient and persistent, and never stop learning and growing in your field.

Chapter 10: Change Your Broke Mindset

| Chapter 10 |

Change Your Broke Mindset

It's easy to get stuck in a broke mindset, where you feel like you'll never have enough money and that financial abundance is out of reach. Changing your mindset to an abundant one can help you attract more wealth and financial success into your life.

Even if you don't believe in wealth manifestation and the energy of money, the reality is that when your mind is completely cluttered with thoughts of being broke and the stress that goes with financial trouble, it doesn't allow the space for new ideas to come to you. By freeing your mind, you will open yourself up to new opportunities and ways of creating wealth.

Here are some tips for shifting your mindset from broke to abundant:

1. Practice Gratitude: One of the most effective ways to cultivate an abundant mindset is to practice gratitude. It's essential to regularly reflect on the things you're grateful for in your life, including the money and resources you do have. This can help you shift your focus from what you don't have to what you do have and attract more abundance into your life. Start by making a habit of writing down three things you're grateful for each day. Over time, you'll notice a significant shift in your mindset towards abundance.

2. Change Your Language: The words we use have a powerful impact on our mindset. Instead of saying "I can't afford it," try saying "I choose not to spend money on that right now." This small shift in language can help you feel more empowered and in control of your finances. This change in language puts you in a position of power rather than being a victim of your financial situation. Speak positively about money and financial abundance, and you'll attract more of it into your life.

3. Visualise Abundance: Spend time each day visualising yourself living an abundant life. Picture yourself achieving your financial goals and having the resources you need to live the life you want. This can help you stay motivated and focused on your financial goals. Visualisation can be a powerful tool in achieving success. By creating a mental image of your desired outcome, you're manifesting it into reality.

4. Focus on Abundance, Not Scarcity: It's easy to fall into the trap of focusing on scarcity and what you don't have. Instead, try to focus on abundance and the opportunities and resources available to you. This can help you feel more optimistic about your financial future. Believe in abundance and know that it's available to everyone who is willing to work for it.

5. Surround Yourself with Abundance: Surrounding yourself with abundance can help you shift your mindset and attract more wealth into your life. This could involve reading books or blogs about personal finance and abundance, attending networking events with successful entrepreneurs, or even just spending time with friends and family members who have a positive and abundant mindset. Being around people who exude a positive financial mindset can be contagious.

Changing your mindset from broke to abundant won't happen overnight, but with consistent effort and practice, you can start to attract more wealth and financial success into your life. By practicing gratitude, changing your language, visualising abundance, focusing on abundance, and surrounding yourself with abundance, you can cultivate a more positive and abundant mindset and start living the life you want. Remember, the key to changing your mindset is to be persistent and patient. Keep at it, and eventually, you'll see results that will help you crush your debt and live the life you want.

Chapter 11: Enjoy Life

| Chapter 11 |

Enjoy Life

As women, we should never feel guilty for indulging ourselves in life's pleasures, whether that be a vacation, a new outfit, or a night out with friends. However, it's important to balance these indulgences with responsible financial planning to avoid unnecessary debt and financial stress. Here are some tips on how to plan a budget-friendly vacation and indulge ourselves in a responsible manner.

Firstly, it's important to identify what's important to us and what we can realistically afford. We don't have to travel in luxury to have a great time, and there are many alternative options that are just as exciting and won't break the bank. By setting a realistic budget and sticking to it, we can enjoy our vacation without the added stress of overspending.

Another way to save money on a vacation is to seek out the best deals available. This can be a fun activity, as it allows us to be creative and resourceful while finding items we need or want at a lower cost. There are many websites and apps that offer discounted travel packages, accommodations, and activities, making it easy to plan an affordable vacation without sacrificing quality.

In addition to seeking out deals, we can also explore non-traditional options for indulging ourselves, such as garage sales, closing-down sales, and online trading platforms. These options offer unique items at a fraction of the cost, allowing us to treat ourselves without overspending. By being resourceful and creative in our indulgences, we can avoid the accumulation of unnecessary debt and maintain our financial stability.

Furthermore, we can generate side income to finance our indulgences. This could involve taking on odd jobs or small projects with the intention of using the money earned to treat ourselves to something special. By taking control of our finances and actively working towards our goals, we can enjoy the fruits of our labour without compromising our financial health.

Finally, it is critical to strike a healthy balance between financial security and personal fulfilment. By being mindful of our spending habits and taking proactive steps to plan for and enjoy life's pleasures within our means, we can achieve this balance and achieve financial freedom. Indulging ourselves should never come at the cost of our financial well-being, and by practising responsible financial planning, we can enjoy the best of both worlds.

Summary

In Summary

Ladies, you did it! You have come to the end of this book and hopefully gained some valuable insights on how to crush your debt and start living the life you want. It takes courage and determination to take control of your finances, and I applaud you for making the effort to do so.

Remember, managing your finances is not a one-time event; it's a lifelong journey. As you continue this journey, there will be ups and downs, and sometimes you may falter. But that's okay, because you now have the tools and knowledge to pick yourself back up and keep moving forwards.

I hope you have learned to embrace the power of budgeting, tracking your expenses, and saving for the future. By being mindful of your spending habits, you can ensure that you stay on track with your financial goals and avoid slipping back into debt.

I also hope you have learned to be kind to yourself and give yourself grace along the way. Sometimes unexpected expenses will come up, or you may make a mistake with your finances. But remember, you are only human, and it's okay to make mistakes. The important thing is to learn from them and keep moving forwards.

As you continue your financial journey, don't forget to celebrate your successes, no matter how small they may seem. Whether it's paying off a credit card or sticking to your budget for the month, take a moment to acknowledge and appreciate your progress. These small wins will motivate you to keep going and reach your bigger financial goals.

Finally, I want to leave you with one last piece of advice. Always remember why you started on this financial journey. Whether it's to become debt-free, save for a down payment on a house, or retire comfortably, hold onto that goal and let it be your driving force. When times get tough, remember your "why" and keep pushing forwards.

So, my fellow financial warriors, go out there and crush your debt, build your savings, and start living the life you want. You got this!

www.ingramcontent.com/pod-product-compliance
Lightning Source LLC
Chambersburg PA
CBHW040247220526
45473CB00001B/396